How to Make Shrunken Heads

MARLA BUCHANAN

ISBN-10: 1500433128
ISBN-13: 978-1500433123

A *shrunken head* is a human head that's been cut-off and specially prepared for use as a trophy, or for ritual or trade purposes. Shrunken head novelties made from rubber or plastic can be purchased online or in shops that cater to Halloween-style décor.

There are also lots of sites and books where you can find instructions on making your own shrunken head from carved and dried apples.

This book isn't one of them. Keep reading to learn how to make a *real* shrunken head—like a native.

Head hunting is the practice of taking and preserving a human head after killing the person. This occurred in many parts of the world, including ancient China, Mesoamerica, India, Japan and Africa, but was only documented in the northwest region of the Amazon rainforest.

Shrunken head or "tsantsa"

In pre-Columbian times the art of shrinking heads was widespread in the Andean area. The only known tribes to have shrunken human heads were the Jivaroan tribes that included the Shuar, Achuar, Huambisa and Aguaruna tribes found in Peru and Ecuador. A shrunken head is called a "tsantsa," by the Shuar.

Shuar warriors

The Quechua Lamistas in Peru

Head hunters of the Upper Amazon in Brazil

The heads of the Montenegrins after they came into conflict with this warrior's tribe.

How to make a shrunken head (tsantsa):

1. Remove the skull from the head. To do this an incision is made on the back of the neck and all of the skin and flesh is removed from the *cranial* (part of the skull that holds the brain) area. The skull is then discarded into a nearby river and left

11

as an offering to Pani, the anaconda.

2. Red seeds are placed underneath the eyelids which are then sewn shut with native fiber.

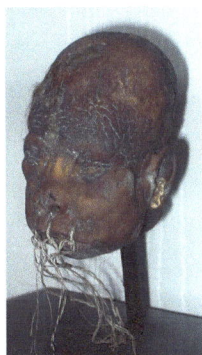

3. Three palm pins are used to hold the mouth together. These will be removed later and replaced with dangling strings.

4. Excess fat is removed from the head and a wooden ball is placed inside in order to help keep the form.

5. The head is then placed in a sacred boiling pot or cooking jar and boiled in water that contains a mixture of herbs that contain *tannins* (substances that help "tan" the skin of the head into leather).

The head is simmered for approximately 1-1/2 – 2 hours (not *too long* or the hair will fall out). The skin is dark and rubbery when the head is removed from the pot and is about 1/3 of its original size.

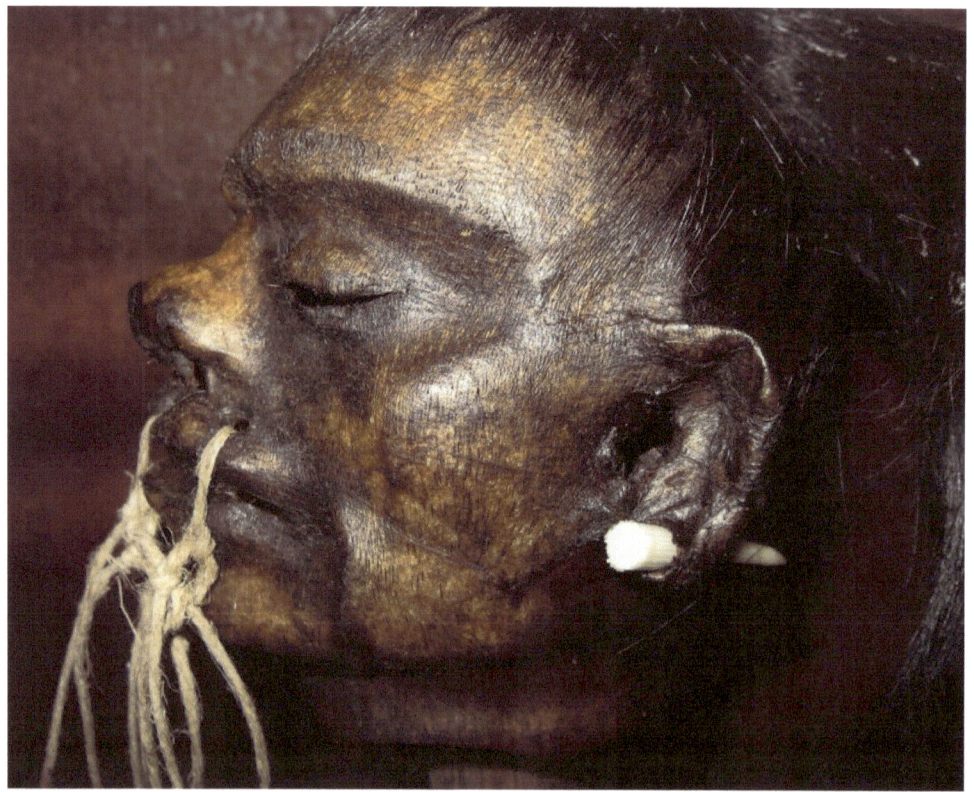

6. The skin is turned inside out and all of the flesh still clinging to it is scraped off with a knife. The

fully scraped skin is then turned right side out and the slit that was originally made in the neck

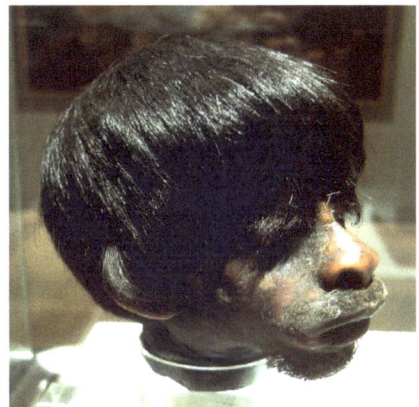

area is sewn up.

7. Hot rocks and sand (that are collected nearby) are used to sear the interior and to help dry and cause final shrinking of the head. The human features are retained and molded in the process. The Jivaroan tribe is especially concerned with realism and the careful preparation of the head in order to maintain the original likeness of the slain victim's face. The heated stones are dropped in one at a time through the opening in the neck and

are constantly moved around inside to prevent the

skin from being scorched.

8. When the skin becomes too small for the stones to move around, sand is heated in a food bowl and substituted for the rocks. The sand enters all of the nooks and crannies of the ears and nose where the heated stones cannot reach. This process is repeated for as long as necessary.

9. Hot stones are applied to the exterior of the face to seal and provide final shape to the features.

10. Excess hair is singed off and the finished product is hung over a fire to blacken and harden. The lips are dried by applying the flat edge of a

heated *machete* (long, flat, sword-like knife) to

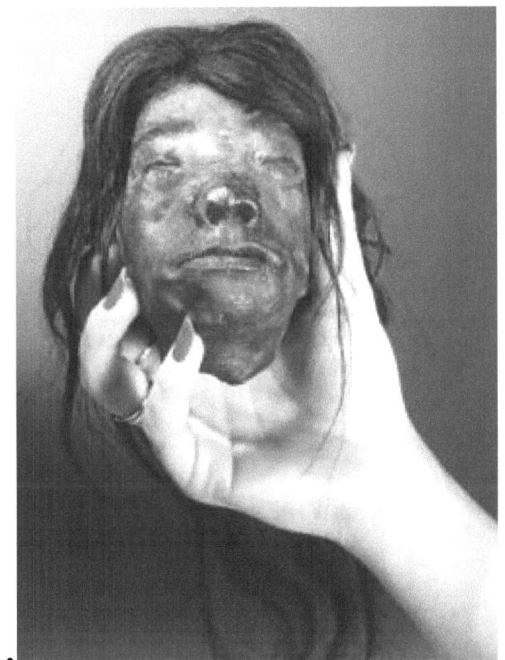

them.

11. The skin is then rubbed down with charcoal ash.

12. The three *chonta* (palm-pegs) are then put through the lips which are then lashed together with string.

13. The head is finally decorated with beads, if desired.

The entire process would last approximately 1 week while the warrior head hunter worked on the head daily while traveling back to his village.

The Shuar and Achuar tribes would follow this process with a series of feasts that centered on important tsantsa celebrations, rituals and ceremonies. These special events would begin on the last day of work on the shrunken head.

The warrior would then make a hole in the top of the head and attach a bit of cord to enable him to wear it around his neck.

Why did they shrink heads? Head hunting and head-shrinking originally had great religious importance.

Shrinking the head of an enemy was believed to capture and control the spirit of that enemy and force him to serve the one who had taken and shrunken his head. It was said that this prevented the victim's soul from avenging his death. The shrunken head was also like a badge of honor to the warrior.

The three main spirits of the Shuar:

1. *Wakani* "soul" of a human which survives their bodily death.
2. *Arutam* "vision" or "power" that protects humans from a violent death.
3. *Muisak* vengeful spirit which surfaces after the murder of a person carrying an arutam spirit.

A muisak was prevented from using its powers by the act of severing an enemy's head and then shrinking it. This process also served as a warning to one's enemies.

Incredibly, immediately after the final celebration the head was often tossed aside with little thought or given to children …

There is nothing better than 'natural,' handmade toys for children. Recycling is the responsible thing to do and is much more eco-friendly than buying some cheap, disposable item made from plastic, don't you think?

Bibliography:

The basic framework for the steps in making a shrunken head was gathered from the following Creative Commons Attribution-ShareAlike source, and the author's knowledge gained through her formal education in anthropology:

http://en.wikipedia.org/wiki/Shrunken_head

http://creativecommons.org/licenses/by-sa/3.0/

Word-of-mouth is crucial for any author to succeed. If you enjoyed this book, please leave a review on Amazon—even if it's just a sentence or two. It would make all the difference and would be very much appreciated.

Thank you.

ABOUT THE AUTHOR

Marla Buchanan is the author of the memoir, **Rescue in Arabia: a true story of abduction, tragedy and hope**, the **Mulberry May Belle** children's book series, and several books of strange and unusual short non-fiction. She is "happily on the doorstep of AARP membership," and a mother of four adult children (and the grandmother of one). She lives in Northern Illinois, and has worked in social services and education. She was married to her Syrian-born ex-husband, Salim Kassem, the father/abductor of their son, Mohamad ("Moe") Kassem, for approximately 6-1/2 years. They were divorced in 1994. In October 2002, Moe was abducted by his father and taken to the Middle-East, where they remained until Salim was killed in a car-rollover in Saudi Arabia, in August 2007. Moe was left critically brain-injured and in a coma. Saudi Prince Muhammad bin Naïf bin Abdul-Aziz Al-Saud, the current Minister of the Interior, and nephew of King Abdullah, personally sponsored Moe's medical care and Marla's travel to, and stay in Saudi Arabia.

 A college graduate, she earned her B.A. in Anthropology (Minor: Women's Studies) at Northern Illinois University, in DeKalb, Illinois, in May 2007, nearly 24 years after obtaining her G.E.D. She was a featured speaker during Women's History Month, at NIU, in March 2007, where she spoke about Moe's abduction, and was also named an "Outstanding Female Student of the Year."

 Marla has traveled extensively throughout the Middle-East and Europe, visiting such countries as Syria, Jordan and Saudi Arabia, as well as England, Switzerland and Italy. She's also a 10-year cancer survivor after having been successfully treated for Papillary Thyroid Cancer in 2004. Recently diagnosed with the genetic movement disorder, Essential Tremor (ET) the author is determined to overcome this most recent challenge via her amazing ability to adapt and change. Her life is an evolutionary work in progress.

(Memoir/4.8 stars) **"Rescue in Arabia: a true story of abduction, tragedy and hope"**

On Saturday, October 12, 2002, 14 year-old Mohamad ("Moe") Kassem was abducted by his Syrian-born father and taken to the Middle-East. In August 2007, his father/abductor was killed along with his step-mother and youngest half-brother, in a car-rollover near Hafr Al-Batn, in Northeastern Saudi Arabia. The accident left Moe critically brain-injured and comatose. Saudi Prince Muhammad bin Naif bin Abdul-Aziz Al-Saud, the current Minister of the Interior and nephew of King Abdullah, personally sponsored Moe's medical care and his mother's travel to, and accommodations in Saudi Arabia. This book chronicles years of child and spousal physical, mental and sexual abuse that culminated in abduction, tragedy and hope.

Available in Kindle and paperback at Amazon.com and Createspace.com.

http://www.amazon.com/dp/B00JUW16XE   https:www.createspace.com/4775674

(Children's fiction/written in verse/5 stars) **"Mulberry May Belle"**

MULBERRY MAY BELLE is not your average eight year-old girl. With friends like 'Tentacled Ted,' who lives in her closet; 'Mr. Mummy,' who visits with her at night, and a ghostly boy named 'Bill,' Mulberry (along with her step-sister, Lonnie) occupies herself with 'scaring' trains via mulberry stains, and playing games on cemetery plains…Wednesday Addams would LOVE her, and you will too.

Available in Kindle and paperback at Amazon.com and Createspace.com

http://www.amazon.com/Mulberry-May-Belle-Marla-Buchanan-ebook/dp/B00KRQ5LUQ/ref=pd_sim_kstore_2?ie=UTF8&refRID=1JWX1RH9C7RYH2MVB11W

https://www.createspace.com/4839356

(Short non-fiction book on decay applied to the fictional zombie genre) **"Zombie Anatomy: The Walking Dead and Decay"**

Everyone knows how to 'kill' a zombie, but do they know how to accurately guess their 'age' based on their appearance and state of decay? This book, written by an author with a B.A. in Anthropology, explains the science of decay (including a "Zombie Timeline of Decay," for reference) in easy to understand language that will help the reader impress their fellow zombie fans with their new-found expertise in zombie anatomy. They'll never watch a zombie movie or T.V. show the same way again!

Available in Kindle or paperback at Amazon.com and Createspace.com.

http://www.amazon.com/dp/B00LCVBPAA https://www.createspace.com/4875643

(Short non-fiction/5 stars) **"Cannibals: Do people taste like chicken?"**

Cannibals—who are they and why do they do what they do? ... What do people actually TASTE LIKE? ... From pre-history to modern times, we'll explore the who's, what's, where's, when's—AND TASTES of cannibalism … Cannibals: Do people taste like chicken? Is "finger lickin' good"—guaranteed!

Available in Kindle and paperback at Amazon.com and Createspace.com.

http://www.amazon.com/dp/B00LHRMJD6 https://www.createspace.com/4882874

AUTHOR'S CONTACT INFO:

FACEBOOK

http://www.facebook.com/rescueinarabia

TWITTER

MarlaBuchanan13

AMAZON AUTHOR'S PAGE

http://www.amazon.com/author/marlabuchanan